CANDY 4 CANNIBALS

For Clive

Jeremy Reed

CANDY 4 CANNIBALS

with Gold Light

Jeremy

ENITHARMON PRESS

First published in 2017
by Enitharmon Press
10 Bury Place
London WC1A 2JL

www.enitharmon.co.uk

Distributed in the UK by
Central Books
50 Freshwater Road
Chadwell Heath, RM8 1RX

Distributed in the USA and Canada
by Independent Publishers Group
814 North Franklin Street
Chicago, IL 60610
USA
www.ipgbooks.com

© Jeremy Reed 2017

ISBN: 978-1-911253-30-3

British Library Cataloguing-in-Publication Data.
A catalogue record for this book is available
from the British Library.

Designed in Albertina by Libanus Press
and printed in Wales by
Gomer Press

For Lee Harwood 1939–2015
With Love

'Everything depends on the energy of the present.'
THOM GUNN

CONTENTS

PERSONALS
    Irene Creaton 13
    White Lilac 14
    Alstroemeria 15
    Pink Day 16
    Habit 17
    Taken My Feet Away 18
    Where Did It Go Bert? 19
    If You Saw Me Now 20
    Reading with Thom Gunn 21
    To Be David 22
    5 Years 23
    The Slide 24
    Caring 25
    My Familiar Junky 26
    Foyles Café 27
    You're Gonna Hear From Me 28
    August 26th (Why?) 29
    Giving it away 30

DO YOU COME HERE OFTEN?
    1984 33
    Do You Come Here Often? 34
    Self-Destruct 35
    Marchmont Street 36
    Leaving It All Behind 37
    The Day Ziggy Died 38
    Gardenia 40
    It's the Same Old Feeling 41
    Robin 42
    Thunder Shock 43
    Time or You Gotta Go 44
    Any Morning 45

ADDICTED
    The Real Deal 49
    Purple Hydrangeas 50
    Soho Out 51
    Store Thieves 52
    Mother's Little Helpers 53
    Addicted 54
    Doctor Stu 55
    Spooky Action 56
    Black Bathroom 57
    Hostas 58

MISTER RIGHT
    Mister Right 61
    Seeing Bill 62
    Mahonia 63
    Missing 64
    Hyacinths 65
    You Can't Catch Death 66
    Days To Go/ Please Don't Go 67
    The Big Sleep 68
    Facing the Wall 69
    Morphine 70
    Night 71

SUNSHINE OF YOUR LOVE
    Sunflower Politics 75
    Gladioli 76
    Pink Morning Glories 77
    Convolvulus 78
    Aquilegia 79
    Black Petunias 80
    Narcissus 81
    Potted 82
    Black Hollyhocks 83
    Huge Red Poppies 84
    Mimosa (You really got me) 85

URBAN GLAMOUR
    Urban Cannibal 89
    Wallis Simpson in the Shower 90
    Andy Flash 91
    From the Bottom Up 92
    Lou Book 93
    You 94
    A Certain Type 95
    Purple Heart 96
    Life 97
    Sticky Toffee Crème brûlée 98
    Bits and Pieces 99
    Spleen after Baudelaire (Cannibal Remix) 100

LAST TANGO
    Doughnut 103
    Red Carpet 104
    Falling Apart 105
    You're Now and Then 106
    Final Audit 107
    You could be Mine all Mine 108
    September Gold 109
    Eliot + 100 110
    Foggy Abstractions 111
    Book Hoarding 112
    No Resting Point (Man, You Gotta Move) 113
    Bordeaux Supérieur 114
    13/2 115
    Z 116
    Going Down 117
    Martyn 118

PERSONALS

IRENE CREATON

You dead: a core part of me deconstructs
like splitting open an apple
a Cox's with a snakeskin rash
on a bricky cheek: so far back
Sand Street, book piles like Lego constructs,
books for obsessives in disordered spills
started me out on my fetish-
issue points, states, the name Irene
soft like the white heather sprays in a glass
on a booked-up table. I was punk obsessed
Lou Reed as liquid gender bad-boy icon
and used to slip into a gay bar
the Side Door's silver-foil bandaged walls
a block away from your regenerated stacks
in a street so seventies anaesthetised
it seemed jabbed by elephant tranquilliser.
Back of the Jersey harbours, most of it smashed out,
your shop was my luck on academy:
book bags delivered in a vintage Daimler
with sliced tomato red upholstery.
Miss you for ever, and the light you shone
on my student holidays lived in your shop
pointing me ways and quietly looking up
the day I brought you brimming white
chrysanthemums.

WHITE LILAC
for Lee Harwood

Flipside to purple, luscious
white tusk, bubbly texture
like Aero Mint
(Japanese have Green Tea brand
and Vanilla Milkshake) – I'm off-
subject; hanging out under
their effusive down-pointing droop
like they're a handle to summer's
determined pistachio sky
churned with airborne pollutants
listed in the *Evening Standard*
and lilacs a Persian immigrant
a 16th century – did it ever exist?
sexy interloper
at Long Acre Covent Garden
pushing its scent forward like time
that never meets the future
and over this wall I've never
patched into my sight before
corroded brick turned burnt-orange
with crumbling fretlined mortar
and these white tumbledown pointers
collapsed into gravity.

ALSTROEMERIA

On Lee's wooden table, placed there as math,
a 5-syllable inclusion
in what occupies this Andean thrust
of colour, rose, orange, purple
Inca lily, parrot lily –
it's sharing sight that matters much as thoughts
and where they click on a dissolve
we're focused on a naked lunch
ideas poised on the end of a fork
between the vegan bite and the green sky
pouring in through his big window.
If you believe a Chinese butterfly's heartbeat
stomps up a hurricane in Florida
wouldn't you, then we're seeing right
these stripy petals as a metaphor
for adding profit to a mood, our time
together dusts one thought to another
like folding a shirt, so much world outside,
and alstroemeria holding it all together.

PINK DAY

They sit as doubles – pink parrot tulips
adjusting to the upbeat light quota
your Brunswick Place big street windows provide
like how the brain scatters its memories
into a hologram – that shocking pink
it's almost violet – a green detail
inclusive to the pigment, do we see
in the same colour, live in the same time
as Battersea consortium for rebuild
and how do raspberry tulips fit with that?
Our afternoons, I'd make a cake with them
if I could mix time as ingredient
with polenta and six botanicals
for flavour. Brighton's just another town
without your second floor, it's recessed tail
your green relaxant bedroom, and the loo
a compact marble sanctuary to switch
into reflective mode – I like that slot
of solo privacy. But our pink day
it's tulip designs I bought on the street
like sharing sunshine, just the two of us
importing every colour variant they show.

HABIT

All my life 2 or 3
poems a day unstoppable
imaginative dependency
on state-altered imagery
like a space programme
worked in microgravity
or my parallel habit
Valium 10mgs
gotta have it, it can't be
diff to my neurology
hallucinated amygdala
damaged almond-shaped car park
torched-up like a Ferrari
at propulsive getaway.
Never failed me, got it right
from a dodgy deviant start
addiction to every day
weird as my reality
poetry as UFO
sightings – do you ever hear me
in book saturation no
got no credibility
outlaw to the whole quango
hate me for originality
writing on bank notes sometimes
to optimise immediacy
on a skinny knee in Leicester Square
do me in eventually.

TAKEN MY FEET AWAY

You're faceless now in the unaccountable
transitioning millions: exhaustive August haze
hanging in like mauve delusional mirage,
you gone it's like lifting ten years
in a backpack to Victoria
light as a biomolecule.
Gatwick Express – the one way back's
only for a person (me)
not a city. And outside, look –
there's stuffed aubergine in a twist
on the classical imam bayildi
fried crackling discs dipped in beetroot purée,
the rustling fritters popping like hot thought
pointy with inspiration, done outdoors.
I wait all day for dark, when it comes on
I can't differentiate black from black
like sorting present from the past – and you
you're unlocatable – last meeting slung
beside the river – couldn't make it through –
and all those moving lights, travelling dazzle
all speeding one way towards Waterloo.

WHERE DID IT GO BERT?

A mulberry (mushy fruits) a laurel tree
slung up a bend away from remade docks
shipping containers painted red oxide
the skyscraper bulk of an orange hull
like a NASA whack of rogue physics
remember it? – I've seen the redesign
dribbles of pink paint where we stood
like a psychotic fatwa
and the harbour like a Lego planet lit
with Day-Glo orange, blue and green
ain't ours, we moved through different times
to get there, mashed up against facts,
like a resurfaced wall. Concrete access ramps
a port's like a military zone.
I'm there an hour, a grainy afternoon visit
to manipulate 20 years lost out
like a snapshot of a snapshot
that's upside down. We came out the wrong side,
but right for us as collusive weirdos
throwing our cans into the tide
knowing they'd peel like us to stripped layers.

IF YOU SAW ME NOW

Cuffing a wet apple's C-cup
in a Hampstead back
a venomous green rain-beady rhomboid
pulling it from its orbit
like a black hole ingests a star
290 m light years away
1984 allusions in my mind
like an end of time brainscan
did whatever it was end then
like a nuked primer-painted car
left scalded beside the highway
a race substituted by mirage men?
Don't know in drizzled illusion
only the spitting cooker in my hand
as plump juicy antagonist
and you'd note my patterned shirt
as blue cornflower design on cream
attention to detail exact
as stitches in a seam
and the preoccupation with futures
a window on tomorrow
that I live in now – imagine
the lot as a poem's light-speed
while I shake green explosive apples down.

READING WITH THOM GUNN

A washed out black skinny T-shirt,
faded charcoal, Med-blue lived-in Levi's,
black leather greaser biker boots,
assertively masculine CA gay,
our only prop Elton John's grand piano

as hulkish architecture in the room,
two skinnies in a capital shock-waved
by viral pandemic, both of us stripped
to poetry, no intros, no apologies,
but done clean as an asparagus spear,

his bullet-proof, smart, economical,
mine streaming sensationalised imagery
writing the street directly on the page.
Thom's *Man with Night Sweats* out, instant winner
as humane documenter of the plague

swiping his small Cole Street community,
his worked out muscle tone, coffee-sunned skin
perfecting fitness, not the crystal meth
he revved into his veins from street dealers
back home, the chemical that kept him thin.

The London Lighthouse, both doing our thing
for fundraising, we talked mostly of rock
backstage, guitar driven stuff and his teens
spent sniffing Hampstead Heath for overview,
dead friends, losses and all the might have beens.

TO BE DAVID

Diagonal lazy gold Bloomsbury light
8 mins travel time from a sun
92 million miles away
arrives in hallucinated rhomboids
on Little Russell Street's bricky
apartment blocks 14/10
the afternoon still as a honey jar's
blond on blond illusory density.
I'm given scared up associations
David Gascoyne's maxxed up
New Collected Poems, those years I knew
his tampered with delusional mind
electro-shocked with neural scars
and mostly lateral thought like dazzle
seen on a plane's wing as it tilts:
he couldn't fix subject, scrambled
the drift like English Breakfast on a plate.
David burnt out at 25
another David
dandified misfit in a chalk-stripe suit
missing out on decades like he slept through
a parallel processed long haul.
I hold him in my hands now as a book
speed up time dipping across his decades
reading the street down towards Gilbert Place
infra-red to ultraviolet wavelengths
reinvent his morning glory blue eyes
cornering something in a private space.

5 YEARS

I see you wrong way round, skinny jacket
black-and-white dogstooth check, a 38,
dematerialising as people do
into an off-Long Acre niche
a transit pathway into Garrick Street.
Five years ago, five forward, it's one time
we threw shapes at each other and your look's
demonstrably skinnier lonelier
acutely disaffected dystopian
like stamping muddy feet over red silk.
Can't catch you bandit and Bowie's Five Years
the glam androgyny still climbs my spine
like freaking into new reality.
We shared the moment from light years away
like the Mayan calendar's end of time
prediction, a crashed flameout asteroid.
Your details, obsessions, daily effort
I got the lot in a dysfunctional shop
you came into, and now you're lost again
cutting diagonals off Floral Street
just as it starts to, starts to, starts to rain.

THE SLIDE

5 years back, is it always five
hexes me self-destructively?
you tubed to meet outside St Martin's Court
casually but too seriously,
messed anorexic thinking I'd undo
your confused sexuality –
you brought me three maroon-black dahlias
with a bitterish chocolate scent
awkwardly maintained for an afternoon
West End getting about – I took you where
I'd got London as epidermal grit
worn it like a suede-elbowed tweed jacket
until it got to me: then underfoot.
You tried to get into me like a dye,
a red virus, red addiction, red squeeze
like strawberry jam, your life was red neon,
mine was a cool tranquillizing blue.
Your father wanted you back in Berlin
sanitised as a lav deodorant cube,
floaty blue not red, you went back, back, back,
leaving your nose-print gummed on my window.

CARING
for Peter

I finger-stab the Pillmate slot
for Sunday's quotient, 9 drugs
to start the day – a heavy truck
inside your arteries
orbiting a roundabout
washed down by apple juice.
Routine's your comfort zone
now you're restricted to a frame
and walk as though you're on the moon
the effort to find oxygen.
2 days with you, it's like a year,
your crunched, cataloguing of obsessions
in which you're always top
of the subsidiary tip –
publishers you've outlived or seen
sucked into the US juicer
licked of all identity like grapefruit.
Your floral shirts out-Hawaii Hawaii
lime, plum, aqua, lurid pink
like mixing a smoothie sunset,
and there's no future that's the worst
just this big window on the past
that's intermittently fogged then clear
with something so close up it's in your face
like miles of sky, a clear blue mile
in which you suddenly see everything.

MY FAMILIAR JUNKY

I see her outside Foyles, corner
of Manette Street coming at me
from 20 light years away
in a heroin galaxy –
'you're wearing makeup ain't you luv'
she quizzes sympathetically
track marks on one exposed black arm
like a graffiti epitaph
carved out of dependency.
She wants change, and I'm vulnerable
to exchanging identities
seeing her need in my own
through navigable empathy.
'You in a band?' she tries again,
knowing I give, it's our routine
a method as it comes on rain
as slow flashy hexagonals
'gimme sugar in my tea'
she says, projecting harder now
looking like she's terminal
as I dig into crumpled jeans
to help facilitate a wrap
mainlined into a collapsed vein
and give too much of too little
as part of our complicity,
a street exchange 'your makeup luv
it really suits you honey.'

FOYLES CAFÉ

Industrial fixtures sheathed in silver foil
as Factory update, Warhol's room
as copy, 1965 in 2015
like time turned silver in a jar:
a Chinese girl in a red plaid mini
fixed to an Apple mini-pad
like pathological hyperfocus
and outside geometric brick solids
as Soho frontiers: a halogen cone
sighting: what if it came to it
a summit in the corner at a bench
over Coke Lite or Raw Food, some crushed end
planned like a re-run of Big Bang
as time-reversed bringing the whole lot down?
You get the Tea Pigs selection
the nylon sachet like a crumpled parachute
immersed in steam, and when the rain comes on
it's like hissy maracas, trillions
of atmospheres smashing down over miles.
Sixth floor location and I'm up on it –
a slice of the world inside and outside,
the girl's black bangs peroxided blonde gold,
her makeup like a pastel candy scoop,
the sunlight quickly coming back again.

YOU'RE GONNA HEAR FROM ME

Maybe one day some foggy day
my algorithm will come up
buying dress rings at Jubilee Market
pink paste and marine turquoise
as an obsessive fetish –

or alleyed off Maiden Lane
in a furred Covent Garden artery
where I found a woman's red shoe
like the one in Bowie's 'Let's Dance'
discarded like a reject

and keep it at home as hoodoo
a size 5 geranium red Bally
as part of what I do
crunch all the bits together
of what I selectively see.

Maybe today's the right day
my chemical signature peaks
instructing you by telepathy
to exit the red Central Line
and pretend you're looking for me

as a pineapple-shaped idea
made into a reality
and we'll go tracking each other
under the radar – you and me
on the Circle Line for ever.

AUGUST 26TH (WHY?)

I write a sonnit on the bathroom wall
black marker pen on bluish-jade
(think Ted Berrigan's Sonnets, note the e)
a fourteen-liner metawar mashed smash
is how I fuck with feng shui:
the day scrambling blue scintillating showers
a scattering of teardrop-shaped diamonds
artefacts of image-capture strobing
the sky like a five-mile wide jellyfish
I gotta snapshot, like slippery purple.
Shakespeare wrote sonnets boozed-up, used-up, sad
at the kitchen table, didn't spoon muesli
with raisins like me, ripped at venison
recreating (re-anatomising) Mr W. H.
and his pink chewy sweet fellatio.
I get back to my marker; shape each word
like fingerprinting brain cells, transient
wash-off: I'll keep a line or two, rebuild
the contents later, when I dye my hair
the colour of a sonnit, bookish blond.

GIVING IT AWAY

My mother's *Natural History of Selborne*
Macmillan & Co 1875
juniper green cloth, gilt decorations,
boards tough as croc skin,
unread, a luxurious fetish,
gilded top edge (book physicals)
600-page personalised block,
a cryogenic object
inherited: a rabbit with deformed teeth
illus p335
like a zombie's interplanetary hop
into alien. Weighs like my Waitrose shopping
transporting it to a friend
like a rectangular swamp reptile
gifted for a Selborne move.
What I lift are the pressed red maple leaves
picked on my mother's visit
like bits of a faded maroon kimono
disintegrated, positioned to keep
like time left fingerprints inside the book
to outlive mother. I let go its weight
to make her death that much lighter
this autumn day, Bury Place, Bloomsbury –
a pinch of gold dust in the dusty violet light.

DO YOU COME HERE OFTEN?

1984

The timeline's always just ahead of tech
as social lubricant, a vectoring
we can't reverse: today I hung around
Southbank Beach getting personal with the Thames
as city avatar – a cold green-grey

psycho dominant, drizzled at low tide
to lazy rhythm, smelled the future there
like soggy jeans, skinned cans, bottles and bolts
littering randomly, a tidal glow
like fuzzy silver hanging on the air.

This moment pebbles orbiting a star
stick together as dusty particles
and over millions of years collect
to form a planet. The Southbank corrodes
like it's locked into 1984

like quarters do – skyline architecture
that seems excerpted from an unnamed war
the one we can't remember that moved on
like a drug lord on a souped motorbike
as vanishing-point. There's a Lovecraft note –

'Man makes appt with an old enemy.
Dies – body keeps appt.' It's like that,
a shadow war, a cloned flameout, no end,
just prospect; and the tide comes back at me
chasing dispersals of its frothy trail.

DO YOU COME HERE OFTEN?

A beach like gold dust – solo footprints there –
a swishy jade-green tidal flux,
a book, a phone, I'm astronaut
on quartzy, grainy regolith,
my exo-planet 1-mile asteroid –

Koko ni yoku kurun desu Ka?
vous venez souvent ici?
that's if I found a stranger there
soluble nationality
unidentifiable genes

engineered from a baked beans can.
A cloudbase pumped up on steroids,
can't get to the top of my emotions
without encounter – a tattoo
done as a purple star cluster

fractionally above left ankle?
Vieni qui spresso?
another summer somersaults
like a planet's tilted orbit
into burnt-out backdated drop.

I've colonised this little bay
hoping you'll walk out of ten years
unchanged – the world reset – a wake
from the future – the fog still in
like a blue mirage slowly turning grey.

SELF-DESTRUCT

The work I do it's like a plane
flown 30 times around the world
decommissioned and broken into parts
by order of a profiteer.
I write my arteries to shot highways

my nerves to a red quasar
no money in this overkill
all my multiple ISBNs
like Nazi-coded number plates
accumulate as dead mass on a shelf

my brain downsized into a block
as documentation of mental twist
like a helical fire escape.
I've always felt this river at my back
like the universe balled into a fist

and polarised hot on my spine.
I'm like a cracked digestive in a pack
fault lines in plain chocolate glaze:
an unreusable Mars rocket
ditched in a scorched mission silo…

I can't repair the damage done,
life goes one way to a red traffic light
that's the last sunset in the brain.
I carry on like it's 20 years back:
the outlook sustained sunshine, later rain.

MARCHMONT STREET

A destination.
My black Chinese sneakers make it so
a syruping of protraction
in getting there

Queen Victoria vermilion
brick blocks adjacent Brunswick
like an artificial brain
Waitrose chipped in

as food hall atrium.
Worked back of it: green shoelaces
like twin tangle isomers
or lace up peppermints

a distractive twizzle
got me through lunch-breaks.
It's a cold shower community
don't take you in

with jade shoelaces
and a poem juicing rhythm
in jinxy biomolecules
like radio silence

on the dark side of the moon
that secret in conception
buy at Waitrose grilled artichokes
like zombie prosthetics

LEAVING IT ALL BEHIND

Earth's noisy with its radio –
signal strength drops after a few light years
into explosive red dust storms
goes blank. What's out there's like Alzheimer's
or some delusional brain jerk

won't ever clarify.
It's a kind of limit case
like friends falling away over decades,
centre-parted hair, matte grey eyes,
do you remember how we lost it all

St James', talking back of mint Fortnums
a word collapsing a building
that's how it felt – no message back again
like sending into space; but you
you're there sucking a green lolly

that looks like Venice, ¾ inch smile,
I keep your name secret as a biscuit
concealed as the last in the pack.
Last time I went home I sat on a pier
to be at the end of new beginnings

looking out into blue unclouded air
for what was there a returnable right
free of commitments, sat all afternoon
a green haze powdering like fingerprints
the clear space in me pouring through like light.

THE DAY ZIGGY DIED

A drizzled gin-fizz London sky,
January in on us, checked in
with mimosa's lemon drenched scent,
and you, one base pair in three billion,
a Bowie gene, can't be re-sent
into tomorrow – aliens die

as expats from a signature star.
You got into the future's skin
as Ziggy, shocked up scarlet hair,
high altitude cheekbones, so thin
a gamine look, a weird pop dare,
zootsuit and boots, a red guitar.

A glam seventies chromosome
morphed to the Thin White Duke, Weimar
dystopian, you gave us Low
like a nomadic avatar,
a pop refugee, size zero,
roaming the world without a home.

A cigarette's a smoking gun,
you scorched your lungs, a habit too
altered the body as a fact;
money, mystique, mirage, you grew
into fame as exploitative act
sold on being big as the sun.

There's hardly a confessional line
unlocks your personality
and yet we think you're Major Tom
a spooky NASA oddity
imported from a freaky zone
as a rock 'n' roll alien.

David Jones you got everything
dollars condense to dialect
'Ashes to Ashes' – money's junk
like Wall Street's coke-smeared intellect
and fetched you up wasted and drunk
not knowing the floor from ceiling.

You soundtracked generations, mine
and everyone's, got there so fast
as spook intelligence, we grew
to think you both the first and last
so optimally on the moment new
you arrived quicker than sunshine.

Now you've gone into the big light
like walking out the studio
without a body into space
perhaps surprised by intense glow
and how your voiceprint leaves no trace
at first, before you hear it right.

GARDENIA

Tricky, reluctant, almost there
like repressed orgasm
this subtropical Hawaii diva
don't always showily do flowers
in my carbon-smeared west-facing window
with sumptuously luxurious scent
that's like espresso mixed with sex
and a tub-dig into pistachio
ice cream – the taste imagined
a gradient higher –
and there's no gardenia called Oscar Wilde
as amazing omission,
but the colour's a Dulux Trade Paint
BS 10815
for slapping on muscular walls:
and it's an extended timeline
anticipating a solo reward
like meeting someone on a delayed flight
the expectation lost in waiting
watching updated boards
and daily I check the ups and downs
of arrival – come on and glow
I tell it – making the future happen
by pretending it's already so.

IT'S THE SAME OLD FEELING

Wet clank of kitchen work, it doesn't change
domestic starting point like granola,
a berry mix, a failed gardenia
with a white riff like meringue cream
lacking potentialised incentive flops
like what I do to restart an affair
submerged beneath paint layers. 'It don't work,
you're serially distracted by pretty'
you threw at me as undertones
the colour coding suggests magnolia and plum
as compatible if your aesthetic's Japanese.
I got the colours wrong, like threat
of incoming space rocks, an asteroid
putting back world economy a thousand years
by ripping collision. I need a year
to re-float my gardenia's scent deluge
and what'll I be then, a year weighs what
in worry lines, still digging granola
or fruit muesli from a dark blue bowl
that's like the dark side of the moon flipped round
into such goodness and vivacity.

ROBIN

I come on and don't see you there,
the room's squeezed, and I work the floor
as poets do, throw
arabesques – you're in your drink
so eloquently, the same glass
as top up from five years ago
that never empties, goes like that
as petrol in the veins,
a dandy in a black fitted coat
with a style gallery you inherit
unpacked from a Marc Bolan trunk
shipped back from the future.
I do a short set, it's my way,
and we've got history
me and you, like a shared flavour
of rainy London days. Your refill goes
to shaping your reality
like oxygen. Your black hair's built by dye
into a collapsed curve. The light attracts
the possibility we change, not age,
and come back on each other with this trust
we're up for it, see out another night
as though tomorrow's late inside your glass.

THUNDER SHOCK

Like maxxed-up fluffy ice cream geekery
unstable cumulonimbus clouds peak
like a tower exploded as a plume
in central London, blackcurrant nose cone
as rainband: (meet you from Hong Kong
inside the build) our one familiar place,
and you're in white, all that ultraviolet
tanned on your arms, a green dragon tattoo
escaped a relaxed shoulderstrap, it's moved
in closer, a sonic shock wave, a tweak
of atmosphere like dropping a guitar
onto a concrete floor, its power
imploding as accidental thunder,
and now it's nearer as you smear
a squirt of green anti-bacterial gel
mid-palm, a sudden thermal expansion,
a pulse that's faster than the speed of sound
impacting cooler air, your eyes lit up
with flickers of reactive fear –
I tell you Selfridges won't be a direct hit,
no lightning walloping the café floor,
that it's an Art Deco sarcophagus,
you're safe, as it comes on like military
directing explosive asymmetric war.

TIME OR YOU GOTTA GO

A day ahead of myself or behind
I'll never know, like a cosmetic bruise
on a girl gang leader
blue smear like poppy dust,
she's got it coded alley martial arts.

It's still there Ed Dorn's *Gunslinger*
fade to the spinal lettering
sunned into orange oxidisation.
It didn't slot in yesterday
but looks time-travelled like a plane

been 40 times around the world.
I'd like a perfect copy of myself
as me, like run the whole planet backwards
in time, uploaded into new
that's me, Ed Dorn and you

back where we started hanging out.
It's all a featureless black cube
Knowing what's now and then:
time's like the colour of money
untraceable, protected

by dye and DNA, subatomic,
this sunline timeline on my shoe
sitting in precise gold angle
to sunshine filming *Gunslinger*
arrived photo-shooting the galaxy.

ANY MORNING

A group shot of greyish parked clouds
like a Facebook map of the world
and smacked into peripheral vision
blue and red totemic lupins:
a helicopter traffic report

happening in viewsight overhead.
Google my interests: patent gene
futures, Marc Almond official,
Battersea Stations 1 and 2
and watch the sky transitioning

from sepia to faded blue.
I meet you later, chocolate eyes
toned up by mint-tinted contacts
a silver fingernail documenting
a timeline that's always moving

into overtaking itself.
Cities smell of dyed-out money
and sunk ozone and broken lives
the damage left in a small flat
like legs broken off a chair.

Couldn't tell you the more I do
the more I want to do, levels
going up in buildings and blood sugar,
Bateman Street for juice, look at it
green as the deepest introspective jade.

ADDICTED

THE REAL DEAL

I sell Plath's *Ariel* after twenty years
Faber first issue 1963
a pyramidal nick in the dj
like a Mars module in dark maroon band.
Sylvia's off-planet Guantanamo pod's

subjugated by orange-coated guards.
Suicides have a separate ID
like an Interpol red notice.
I'll join them one day, kick into white surf
and keep walking like I'm meeting a friend.

I didn't ask nothing and got nothing,
life's like that; Sylvia dreamt of glam –
a pink Cadillac roadster 1952,
a Quant dress, earrings like a Wall Street hike,
a glamorised Vidal Sassoon hairdo.

Ambivalent about the sell
I think back times I sold as fantasy
my body, nothing approved in the sale
but resentment both sides – you needing me
me blanking you like a dumb wall.

What'll I buy from selling Sylvia,
nothing useful, just self-indulgent things
making sadness more tolerable, shopping
as kicks-reward – I know the book by heart
like the weight of a familiar green ring.

PURPLE HYDRANGEAS

Near Rue de L'Enfer: I'm thinking Rimbaud
the teen punk and hallucinated poetry –
piss in the rain and a rainbow comes back
black as an aubergine or black piano,
a slammed-up car-stop sighting phone snapshot
but more the saturated aesthetic
some sapphire, cyan petalled snowball heads
Jersey hydrangeas, but thunder purple,
the shock of mutant genus, violet too,
3.31 pm; Rimbaud blew up
poetry's quarantine orbit
like an obscenely venomous bandit –
right on the frontline anti-literary.
Purple hydrangeas, and I nick a bloom,
snapping the stem, singularly selected,
the only one, the fast instinctive swipe,
big purple, got it as a snicky grab,
a bad boy plunder, while you rev the car
for re-routing networking country lanes
like Rimbaud legged, the faster that you walk
the closer you get to the furthest star.

SOHO OUT

On Meard Street I go blank
as a titanium tile
withdrawal
abstract destabilising wobble
I think Sebastian Horsley
a cardiac arrest OD
and note a lime green diagram
of mangoes like 3D teardrops
magnified to mango size
luminous with their own reality.
John Pearse's solo focus –
a raspberry shirt on display
looks like a windowed sorbet
size 15" I conjecture
or yesterday's cerise sunset
that wouldn't go away.
I navigate my way to Dean
parked cars like Martian rovers
on techy blue Mars
and a guy tentatively approaches
tells me he's seen me perform
in converted stables near Russell Square
and all I want is Valium
and won't and wait out waves of fear
islanded in Patisserie Valerie
where even the air seems too near.

STORE THIEVES

Tricky finger poetry
like touching something on the dash
you didn't see, wonky geometrics
slippery as gelatine
in lending objects micro-gravity

displacement from A to B
with asymmetric dexterity.
She couldn't put that together
mid-store, foggy with Paracetamol,
blue oversize Disney eyes face-spotting

prospective customers moon-walking by –
she never saw the object go
so fast it seemed autonomous
a time-slip trickster's telepathic lift
hot as a Boeing's orange exhaust glow.

She doesn't know re-sewn interiors
or stratospheric dopamine rush,
sightings that see round corners, eyes
that fingerprint their target brown or grey
in trancy communal Debenham's crush.

Her headache gets a silver dazzle rinse:
the way things disappear, compacted fit
she can't work out and done right in her face,
left hand, right hand, the movement occupies
peculiar maths across the shortest space.

MOTHER'S LITTLE HELPERS

My doctor, Ian Pitter's aqua eyes,
car paint cerulean, blue view
from the International Space Station out
into orbital blue, spatialized ways
to help me thru before uni,

my scrambled nerves, alienation
from boxy small town scrutiny:
I'd read Burroughs, wore eyeliner
and didn't fit, asymmetric lifestyle
working on confused sexuality

and got dosed by this futures man
with tranquillizing weaponry
the up/down synchronicity
of Valium altered my life
a benzo vision blued reality

and update uppers kicked in too.
He bought me time and got cautioned
for pirate sex. When he talked books
he got me on compass: Lou Reed
was my cool soundtrack to get attitude.

My blues were pharmaceuticals
locking me into couldn't care
down by the docks, a pill in hand
secure, and Ian as my avatar
there once a week to understand.

ADDICTED

I couldn't get you out of my life
bright as a lemony sun-dipped Chablis
as imaginary milligrams
but dark-side in reality
black as generic Chinese hair –

you worked on me sublingually
like Astra Zenica
got you into my tired bloodstream
like bits of poetry
chipped like a nibbled pill's white hub

to coating depletion.
All those mismanaged energies
fizzed into something volatile
like cherry-red Polish vodka
Wisniowka 30% obj.

Couldn't get the poison out,
needed it like a habit
you as internalised identity
so different when the real you burnt
like a can popped in a fire.

Can't let it go it does me in
dependency, you sitting on the floor
demanding I go and I stay
big orange sun in the window
like any other emotion-squeezed day.

DOCTOR STU

He's our type, designer citrus squirty
could be fade on Miller Harris
atomised as ambient residue
he's back from Goa Dr Stu
late as he travels in parallel time

like aviation espionage
building his own day as a Stu unit
like white custom-printed wallpaper
on which he reads his meeting-points
on the 14 in from Fulham

counterintuitively congested.
Nasally clipped vernacular
a 50s dive-speak rebranded
as muffled, tone like a parked car
cooling in an underground bay,

don't make much effort to correct
if you don't get it. Got them enveloped
silver-backed foils of counterfeit Valium
like equidistant planet pops
white as a white-tiled gym.

He's quantum-brief and moving place
before he's yours, price prearranged,
leaving a lick of scent fetish
for which like him I haven't got a name
but hangs on as elusive quizzy trace.

SPOOKY ACTION

Knew this man called Junky Jim
superthin as neon-argon atmosphere
on Mercury's black rock
decorated disposable needles
with stick-on tattoos, red hearts and daggers,
black undulating spearhead snakes,
a skull and crossbones, a barrel fetish
shooting up H. mainlining junk
incisively as a pilot
doing a cockpit check before take off.
Jim who stood outside time, time needs repair,
he'd say, don't take on the future,
stay in the present's shimmer,
smack evolves alternative metabolisms.
His intelligence was the drug,
no overlap: paraphernalia
and all its informatics,
first got on at Portobello, habit
without an exit, taught me things
like singularity and compression
and undivided focus, edit out
what's unimportant, like he found a vein
as pathway to dopamine rush
and drove into the centre of the world.

BLACK BATHROOM

In St John's Wood, specific (Loudoun Road)
I keep the memory like a red dwarf
with its planetary code
and you'd done art dealing and done it all
lugubrious entrepreneurial kill,
wore Habit Rouge, I got it at first sniff
sharing sophistication at pickup –
exchanges in the rain seemed tropical
first year in London when you learn to sell
in ways you don't forget, to win.
And you were Alan, could be anyone
as fucked-up spreadsheet demimonde punter
with just before sunset dyed red hair
and with a nervously alone future.
'Please stay,' you kept on as reprise
like a familiar pop phrase. Black bathroom
ebony faux-marble, so black on black
it seemed like a ceramic piano-top,
gold handled taps, a bottle of vodka
on a bath-side module, it stays with me,
not Alan, that fake Hollywood sarcophagus
sunk like a retrofit in memory.

HOSTAS

Giboshi if you go Japanese –
sumptuously polished leaves like car leather
35–45cm
accessorised audacity
striped like a green backbeat boating blazer
the bluish-lavender September flower
noticeable only to detail snoops
(picked up by William Gibson's *The Peripheral*)
and me backstoried into flower espionage
at Regent's Park aware of their obtuse
north-east Asian startup from car countries,
China, Korea, Japan: bad boy image
pursuing me – I got this sort of pact
with glossy undercover attention seekers
like hostas, and your lusciously mauve bra
purchased at Selfridges reported on the flower's
partially concealed personality
our studio flat flooded by expensive light
smudged in over W1's cloudy glitter.

MISTER RIGHT

(in memory of Bill Franks)

MISTER RIGHT

I do my bit with ruffled peonies,
water them right, these pink Asian tumbles,
thinking of you Bill and your deepening
into compassion, distinctly London
picked-up experience, capital affairs

pulled from the West End's generic corral
of edge-walkers, what you called sensitives,
same-sex attracted, non-scene, soft movers
who came by you, we meet the ones we need
by accident in 12 million stressed lives

surfacing out the tube atlas each day.
I never knew you get character wrong
in terms of seeing hurt as signature
to being special, like shyness rewrites
a hidden kindness, and these spilled peonies

get coaxed into pink focus by the sun.
To me, first meeting, you were Mister Right,
the city in you like an investment
in transitioning decades, earlier
we'd have been lovers, later we were friends

who loved each other, optimised shared time
through every illness driven in your cells
as undercover guerrilla attack,
pushing sympathies forward – what was it
a favourite oatmeal jumper you wished back?

SEEING BILL

I want to tell you Bill, surname attached
(Bill Franks), it's only on your red-rugged floor
10 Peninsula Heights that I give up
compressed London stress; the river outside
rolling olive green over eau-de-nil

the stretchy reach from Lambeth to Vauxhall,
the window spotted like a ribbed condom
with anatomised rain, beady columns
like reading a Japanese paperback
in silver characters, a blue police tug

chugging upriver at a cruisy lick.
Bill does the kitchen while I fit into
my favourite sofa-space, 8 years the same
familiarity – I need this place
as my domestic personality,

the flower extravaganza centrepiece
explosive stargazers, pink carnations,
booze on the piano top – I fine-tune there,
de-stress, adapt, decommission the book
that's booting in my cells, adopt Bill-time

as spatialized reality, our own
with M&S Gold Label tea, condensed focus
on capital affairs like a mood-board
Bill colours, mesh with the city that deep
disused tube stations walk into the room.

The outlook's drizzled: let me tell you Bill
surname attached (Bill Franks), I couldn't live
without our ginger snap reprieves, three weeks
as maximum, and all that light we share
bigger than sunlight called back to the room.

MAHONIA

Victoria Tower Gardens, slashing whiff
of drenched lemony early January
yellow twizzles, a swipe that pulls me up
in scrambled sensory attack –
the associations like martini
partial acute bittersweet
randomised bullet-points in memory,
the river ripping power the other side
brown Thames with its turbo-velocity
reprogramming the city's DNA
in hissy chops. I lean over a wall:
somebody's metal detector hoovers
shingle for gold – a blue tug rocks on swell
MERCEDES – bold sans serif tidal roll.
I click on scent like downloading its strands
into a sorted singularity
a sniffy critic tang, move on again
zoning across the bridge – it goes like this
a little sweetness comes attached to pain.

MISSING

Johnny just up and went, dis-
informed, dematerialised, a teen's
beat up vulnerability
(saw his photo in *Metro*)
a demeaned abused runaway
no juice in his juju's
bad luck, and the dead
get stripped of identity,
you Bill as a name without physicals
atomized into viral dust,
particled in your capital
as floaty grainy molecules
over disjunctive drizzly Golder's Green.
No chance of you happening again
not as individuated Bill
you're discontinuous as Johnny
last imaged at King's Cross concourse
as a loitering transient
on spooky randomised footage
dead now or robbing for crack.
And Bill's a reconstructed diagram
all those recreated angles
to convert him into someone
light as the weightless zero-mass of thought
substituting for the man
I live with now as dispersal
who would have taken in Johnny
and selflessly asked for nothing at all.

HYACINTHS

Bought for Bill faux-Deco hairdos
B-girl lives pulled from a bucket
5 in a nude rubber band
maintained round onion-green waists
like you catapult a mini-rocket

into compressed domestic space.
Part blue part lavender thrown tones
from a Pantone chart, indigo
in Bill's Vauxhall crypto-kitchen
the ginger bics cyclindered in a tower

a fault line apparent diagonally
from compressed packing at the top.
How do we get mauve showies rock
on a crystal rim – the new again
like they're grouped around a bus stop

and liberated into dance.
Indoors we sight out Lambeth Bridge
the river moonstone blue and brown
a helicopter's slicing blades
doing vaporous egg-whisks in low cloud

over Millbank, the marine in the light
a foggy aquamarine rolled in dust
(my sighting) Bill resorts the vamps,
the purple in the lavender arrests,
and pitted in mauve you get cobalt.

My gift comes up shine, complements a mood
we keep sustainable like the rip-tide
pushing a rapid groove to Waterloo
under the bridges – thunder in its tracks
and spot on boats that shiver into view.

YOU CAN'T CATCH DEATH

Hexagonal parabolas of blowy snow –
a Russian diagram at Hammersmith
visiting Bill – he knows he's terminal –
what use my pouty blue anemones,
distractive, superfluous frilly works

stuck in a Starbuck's cup as compromise,
there's no vases on oncology wards
and time seems compacted to grapefruit size
a pink fruit we pass hand to hand, don't slice
for fear the interior's all we've got

the ruby segments vivacious with juice.
You a style sultan wear a blue bathrobe,
no dressing up, but remark small detail,
cloth-covered buttons, my black jacket's fit
the way you sold them into mod retail

the vent opening to a red silk fan
of ostentatious exorbitant lining.
I have to so focus present affairs
without a future, verbal scaffolders
doing step-changes that my moonstone ring's

brief talking point – and how do I transfer
an optimistic bite on tomorrow?
I try to be you as you see me go
free for today, and leave you terrified
watching blue diamonds dab at the window.

DAYS TO GO/ PLEASE DON'T GO

Your bed, brown river to the left focused
on a dandified John Stephen blow-up
sliced time-frame 1965
as though he's the pathway to your future
as quantum what, a streaming energy
projectively pushing you out of time
to rehabilitate inside a warp?
Days to go, you wanted the big shot then,
felt toxic as chemical waste, leakage
from badlands. And the song we played
Cat Steven's 'Morning Has Broken'
fragile as a gold brushstroke on the day
stays as inimitable vocal sign
on those optimised optimistic moments
we hoped you'd make it into remission
another time. There's no direction home
without the body, nearer Vauxhall Bridge,
Nine Elms Lane stayed physical geography
fixtured into consciousness. Who could know
your troubled bottom-line, we have our own,
nobody reaches same level down there.
A red bus making tracks to Waterloo
seemed normal, so too the gold dazzling light
amazing, dusted directly from source
so gold the colour seemed exactly right.

THE BIG SLEEP

Back home, the cancer driven through your cells
like the green river's rush towards Lambeth
outside the window, and you keep your hand
over your liver (it's the final cause),
the toxic gateway, no drug referrals
or cellular reversals, just a week,
maximum two. This camp doctor friend with red hair,
your consultant, a skinny-type like me
directs smart humour when he wants to cry
at how the pain revs out of management.
He's Mark, and mother to your helplessness
in our small group of watchers, three of us
compressed into sticky anxiety
at you tubed up into alternatives
of hydration and intravenous drips.
The window frames Whitehall's black granite blocks,
the jackal's fortress, nearer a red crane
works a still partially constructed tower
and right on looking there's a shower of rain.
For Bill, time's shut down, and he's parallel
to us, in hallucinated zones, then pushed out
to mesh with bits of our apparent reality.
I leave the room for Mark's factual recall,
it's only days, and note again the pink
chrysanthemums splashed on a Chinese vase
meant for Bill's ashes stationed in the hall.

FACING THE WALL

He'll never dress again, but notes my shirt's
Liberty pattern, and the heart-shaped ring
I fit on his left little finger hurts

knowing he'll die with it, a blue opal
I pulled from Jubilee Market, the red
and green impulses starting to signal

like traffic lights sequenced in foggy grey.
Bill's in the tunnel and there's no way back –
the red signposting indicates delay

before he checks into departure gate.
The happy pills optimise brief surges
of lucid calm and a drip rehydrates

a body that rejects most everything.
He tells me he keeps asking for a shot
to end the pain because it's increasing

all over in distress he can't contain.
I look distractively at the window's
loopy holograph of progressive rain.

I can't believe my friend's torched by his cells,
their mismanagement streaming through his blood,
his taste so toxic the saliva feels

like poison, and there's no weight in his hand
the feeling gone. He turns to face the wall
a way of cutting out I understand.

MORPHINE

The big sleep starts and I can't reach you now
the drug's mismanaged messages
hallucinating your reality
into a time-slipped streaming video,
your great love John Stephen as a blow-up

staring you down from 1965
into the present, a His Clothes photo
optimised, dandified, fixed on the wall
comforter with no power at all
to alter how cancer accelerates

through every pathway, you're too weak to sit
and in your vulnerability beautiful,
your body shampooed and your silver hair
still springy, as you take another hit
from an agency nurse and turn away

to feel your way around the pain
that has no boundaries but builds attack
that scrunches you into a crumpled ball.
I ask under my breath an end to this
and back out to recover in the hall.

You're rehabilitated for a time
to clarify then sucked under into
no differentials but a broken sleep
from which you wake asking what you've done bad
before your panicked state gets dragged down deep

and there's no coming back, just an alert
it's ending, a last struggle at the drop
into terminal blackout and outside
it's dark – the London Eye like a UFO
spinning its coloured lights above the tide.

NIGHT

You disappeared by our time 3am
no recognisable Bill personality
clicking on as inimitably you.
I hope you time-slipped back to 1966
orange euphoric apogee
on your trajectory through night pathways
out of your body as city, the capital
you lived as psychogeography
all those years niched in a peacock barrio
Carnaby Street's dandified hip, you there
and there with John. You gave me history,
a personalised focus on London years
I didn't live, coloured retro-anthology
of individuals cutting it –
your sixties Rolls and purple Cadillac
instances of that, slices of chopped time
held together by bacon rolls and tea
for natural simplicity. Now you've gone
do you remember any signposting
familiar to the London you knew
or kept on growing into as knowledge
sitting in centre of it, each address
a floor above expectation, the top
the last you knew out over the river's
green muddy gravitational pull.
We've lost all contact now, but I cut thoughts
like Bill-shaped diamonds to connect
with possibilities of who you are
lying abandoned in the mortuary.

SUNSHINE OF YOUR LOVE

SUNFLOWER POLITICS

Lemon flop-heads on sticks
an omelette with a black hub
on cartel-grade tyres
with heliocentric politics
they're kinda avatars
like the Beatles returned
all four from the dead
in 2030
for a rooftop redo
and maybe they sense orbiting debris
on light-sensitive sensors
and what goes on with red giants
and their expiry dates
like Kepler-56b
130 million years on
in the dusty smashed up cosmic backyard.
They're no scent for my sensory
scent-addicted radar
just militantly dominant
up there solar overdrive
and there's 8 in convention
as I watch fins drone over
thru marshmallow alto-cumulus
streaming hot kerosene vapour.

GLADIOLI

Amazing red or white camp scroll
think early pre-depressant Morrissey
(associative metaphor)
and briefly I'm on South Bank pop-up beach
gold-grey meniscus reclaimed by the tide
as import/export
debris strip, like old world Kodak
Tri-X panchromatic 35mm film
grey grainy like Morrissey?
A poet's day is mobile, got my theme
like contactless, a touch I'm there,
the Festival Hall blocked behind my back
like a concrete filling, a surf ruffle
collapsing, reassembling, recollapsed
20 metres away. I got it now
my subject for the day – gladioli
like orange chopstick repositioning,
oddly a chic bract, ostentatious swish
I'll buy later to match up with my take
written in range of cold greenish Thames wash.

PINK MORNING GLORIES

Hot raspberry psychotropics
like a kimono's slashed pattern
get my attention like a fold
of foreign bills with hologrammic strips
smelling of Istanbul, Dubai
wavy with glittering amnesia.
Their quotient pulls me abrupt
into mutant frequency
you're taking me back to a six bedroom
prewar build in Brondesbury
I visualise as a Victoria sponge
untouched by time and empty still
like buildings on the moon.
You retrofit bits, I go pink
in watching, like I slice a billion
tiny shifts of culture into
redos – I call poetry.
You're out of time, don't notice how
these hotties aren't the peacock blue
predictables and that town stack
you wish the family hadn't sold
stays in you as acquisitive
bad luck you can't ever let go.

CONVOLVULUS

Off-white UFO formation,
bitter scented, smell like rain
settling after stoked thunder,
same gene as morning glory's
peacock pigment, total blue
like a middle-distance transect
of turquoise sky; but flopped saucers
light-sensitive going up
somewhere that's a limit
to their radar
why do flowers ever stop
they could be brutalist skyscrapers
outdoing the curtained Shard,
but these stay level with their thrust
to make it up a garden wall
as green-eyed confection
nose-up to smoky sunshine
while I interrogate their look
as empty calories
doing spatial navigation
address the poem they invite
by graduated patterns
seeing as the way I write

AQUILEGIA

Holly's eyes on them bi-colours
pink lemonade-pink
white dollop, or purple quintuple spike
like a messed reactive hairdo
on someone I knew
glam as their differential.
You can mix the flowers in salad
(the root's cardiogenic toxic)
they remind me today not tomorrow
of big nursery-style numbers
written up on campus blocks
in my time at Wivenhoe Park.
They're in a space between a space
and named only when seen
sound like a spirit brand
a flavoured Polish vodka
a word like sandwich filler
if it's not in your life
with its number 5 for 5 syllables
aq ui leg ia
like calling a lover
over and over
before they reappear

BLACK PETUNIAS

Didn't anticipate you'd
saturated no-colour black
like rush-hour bobs on the Tokyo subway
there like black shock or an object stolen
inexplicably stolen back
as confrontation, didn't expect you'd
and me visiting, black flowers like wine poured
with a dexterous twist you'd
left the garage door open, its fig smell
syrupy ambivalent, like the bike's
money-repro Lambretta
on its pegs under an orange halogen.
Black pulls me in like meditation
separating from busy to blank
into floaty concentration
and flat black horny petunias
didn't expect you'd
cultivate anomolous you
pointed to like inky paranormals

NARCISSUS

A mashed orange sunset as eye
like the furious aurora
behind a rocket as latest news
around the system: cold effusive scent
like a stiffly pressed white shirt –
or would you believe it vodka
tinted with a mixer
into alcoholic whiffy higher state
slammed cocktail alterer.
Suddenly they're there rehearsing
vertical yogic posture
in April cool like an opal
polished on the sky's blue curve
and these stumped clusters are local
all down the street NW3
like a London brand a can
with your private data printed out
on a peeling label –
and later the kitchen window
like I'm looking out backwards into time
and again their off-white frills
randomise a yard radius
in on my view my look
like a galaxy stuffed with wonky moons.

POTTED

5 in a 5-inch pot
an iris moment indigo and gold
like a tongue of Turkish carpet
licking a pinewood floor
in lysergic arabesques
they're like early flight arrivals
confused in purple loping scarves
got in disoriented
with endocrine fuzzy jet lag
and we're behind in January
a thought back instead of ahead
the cold delaying rhythm –
I'd rather stay in bed
reading William Gibson
in a black wool pixie's hat
my thundery lipped iris
making extravagant figures
in dotty ballet shoes
so odd you couldn't make them out
for pattern, just casually note
their presence like we do a rug
sighting its rubies trodden underfoot.

BLACK HOLLYHOCKS

Chocolate maroon/ beetrooty
then black as a Chinese bob
brattish punky 7ft spikes
full on like a demographic marker –
at Ridge Road, upper Haringey
cloud level like walking on thunder
and W.D.M. (white dead men)
assaulted in black on a wall
and the atmosphere's like a lav mirror
1st class on a Boeing 777
too refractively reflective
like a hologrammic foil,
above London it's crazy physics
and black hollyhocks sit the mood
Nigra if you're smart botanist
or know a black push-up bra
or how to load into your cortex
something black found in a car
and over the dip there's Crouch End
that kinda smells of coffee
black black black
as a black shock hollyhock

HUGE RED POPPIES

The first pop – a frilly red parachute
puffed into shivers by breezy grammar
unopened testicular heads
glowering bluely blackly for a week
like missiles stacked in a silo
and opportunistically tweaked by light
into brutalist hairy skyscrapers
intense flamenco red ostentation
a dusty silk fist as a flower.
Another day there's five I count
with amazing purple centres, violet
if I go down a tone, a colour shock
holding me to their radius
like red excludes every other colour
for happening fast. I lose it all
the sense of other things, diversity,
like vision's an upfront ten feet
downsized universe, all I've got
with no inclusions, just six red poppies
overspilling into a giant China-red sun.

MIMOSA (YOU REALLY GOT ME)

Shock of lemony torched-up scentheads
windy pompoms doing chord-changes
vectored into random groupings
didn't know it was opopanax
used by scent mixologists
the thing slung over a parallel wall
back of me same zip code
so loud it's psychedelic – I get ten
maybe 15 sightings a day
to assimilate its motives
according to (me) in the wrong time-zone
to know real reality:
and I had it once Mimosa cocktail
brut champagne with orange bitters
tincture of Grand Marnier
topped by a strawberry for aesthetic
more lurid orange than yellow
but branded mimosa
like I drank the idea of what I remembered
back of the house two weeks or three
as a singular showy exuberance.

URBAN GLAMOUR

URBAN CANNIBAL

A slab of black ceramic subway tiles
noirish monochrome, a black claw-fit tub,
a black mortuary, Dombracht shower head,
didn't expect it, less your bite
a bluish child's heart on my throat
like a micro-salami slice
of discoloured vesicles. Didn't know
your fetish like a sandwich choice
(mine's a Pret humous and salad),
your's human tissue, man on man
in a third-floor apartment Jermyn Street,
red insulated hotel carpeting
lights dipped like an aircraft cabin – and me
I'm not an escort just sophisticate
pulled nonchalantly from the street, someone
curious how looks convert into money
for easy options. Write it down later,
moodboard for cannibals, strategic bites
dished on my body, no other access
requested, just five small geographies
mapped on my body by your cold design
to leave behind traces of your excess.

WALLIS SIMPSON IN THE SHOWER

Levering the Italian chrome head
to shattering foci of stinging bursts
she's peachy with Eddie's love-bites, the fade
of cannibalistic stop-shorts
as blotchy liplines. What's it all about

champagne for breakfast in a tub
as glam rock duchess, nympho-
celeb so loaded with Cartier rocks
she's a loopy Wall Street on heels
a Garrard's flashy jewel re-do

on magnolia-skinned curves.
There's dirt in her artery walls,
I mean networking hike, the sleaze
that fingerprints the real Bessie,
the dupe who got fucked in Shanghai

as studied sexual eloquence
and learnt the menu Eddie gets
as fingertip algorithm.
Neuilly-sur-Seine – she'd like some rough
positioned up against a wall,

only it's lunch at the Savoy
with bubbles doing rope tricks in a glass
the present full of cake filler
and all that emptiness like a curved space
filling tomorrow on another star.

ANDY FLASH

Platinum prototype
made the name modern as big city light
and same-sex cool in a white Tee
and middle-blue Levis
(what blue?) scrubbed lapis lazuli
jeans get their generational blue
pre-washed or thundery
but never Andy's tumbled blue
pressed to one-day creases
and the Andy I knew duped me
of money – mean to a poet
upsets the alphabet
scrambles its resonance
like an exhaust muffler
a fracture on my breath
a dent in my language
I restabilised
but that Andy was bad craft
tricky like a crowd face
you think you recognise
and don't but meet the look
much like the sunglassed art geek
in Levi's and leather jacket
what did I say (scrubbed lapis lazuli)
logo above the back pocket

FROM THE BOTTOM UP

My energy torque – it comes from the street
opportunistic academy
quantifying looks – you and me
and you in public domain – friends by chance
or initialised by money
and all the chopstick repositioning
as detail fetishist of what I see.
Sky's what: Normandy grey and Cupboard green
79 and 201 on Little Greene Colour Chart
and colour of a hazy urban day
Hick's blue 208 by afternoon
with red scrambling like a forked tomato
gutted across a breakfast plate.
Something fifty years into the future
goes by like a dark object – it's you back
in my life – bumped into – no other way
to meet in the city's 12 million
like rain hitting a flat skylight – bang bang.

LOU BOOK

The dust jacket's Factory silver
cover of Andy Warhol's hair
or platinum plane paint
equalised by altitude
or Lou's 'I'll Be Your Mirror'
in which he's now a hologram
an altered psychic sender
doing telepathic tai chi
like people do in opium wars
over violet poppies
with psychotropic juice
and in my book Lou's Earth age
seems like Blake's Enitharmon
1,800 years
compressed into dissident noise,
like he's in the back draft
of something straining to take off
into silver vanishing point.
I gift my author's copies
as a slab of frozen time
January to June went missing
like a radar-invisible
low-slung black vehicle
parked up in heavy duty fog.
I'm never free of Lou
though, habituated to his sound
like the mind turns banana-shaped
at each aggressive sonic bend.

YOU

You in your pointy
grey wool pixie triangular hat
and blacker than black
retro bob (a Mary Quant)
attract and fascinate by looks
shyly introspectively sensitive
a facial masterpiece
to a poet, my 40 books
collapsed into a single flower
at eye-contact with you.
December outside, foggy arcs
like loneliness, I write all day
in need of company
I'm sad and blue
and addicted to poetry.
I'd give you a blue thought a green
and you'd return hot pink or violet –
I know somewhere you understand
my alienation – creativity
I place my thoughts like footprints on a beach
inside the networking lines of your hand.

A CERTAIN TYPE

A weirdo chromosome
like a one in ten billion asteroid
orbital resonance – got it
and never copied
no brat to clone my name
like skinning an orange,
or a car chase purchasing power
as dominant, biffed bodywork.
Kicked into the air prefer
solo, last of my line
like a street that ends in a wall
slashed with neon-pink graffiti
no getting above it.
Most of my friends are samies
doing it once and once only
so individually formatted
one time like a saucer-shaped blue poppy
petals dusted off by the wind
into random, couldn't care
for signature progeny
or leaving a trace of ever
having sat out this cherry blossom day
on a pavement watching it go
time and pink bunchy clusters blown away.

PURPLE HEART

Left pocket of your stonewashed Lee
over the curve, a purple heart
like a customised teardrop
morphed into a dwarf iris
an externally stitched tattoo

as denim incunabula
or a hieroglyphic earring
if you go for big purple.
First of the year indigo hyacinths
stuffed in a label-stripped coffee jar

do sensory quotia
like slicing lemon loaf
and biting it into a swastika.
January's like sitting on a train
opposite to its direction

the air left in the bedroom
could be last year's hangover
we'll never know getting ahead
one milligram one millimetre
your purple moment importing

a neon impulse from my look
breaking the year's barriers
again, like tripping over time
as a restart, a subtle pull
towards the purple bite of your logo.

LIFE

It's further than Centauras A
and close up as your killer startle line
a MAC shock red lipstick bullet's
textured sexy ID as hot –
I never knew Lou Reed omitting slang

from Velvet's classics so they wouldn't date,
only 26 dollars in my hand
as dealer's price for heroin.
I think I'm quickest, but I'm always late
behind ahead. I drink to get it right.

A mobile phone can alter a plane's speed
overriding security software.
I can't get into my rhythm like that
to distort time – I want tomorrow back
before its even registered today.

In China Town, this blond-haired Cantonese
traffics illegal cigarettes, no gap
between her hand and bag it's done so fast
illicit contact, as she pockets cash,
the speed of life compacted in her fist.

What's it I miss, because it's happening
right now, like dusted cappuccino froth
whisked by a lip the moment's travelling,
and Chinese cigarettes, she's sold the lot,
her grab hand topped by a cheap rhinestone ring.

STICKY TOFFEE CRÈME BRÛLÉE

Your fave, you tell me, fisting hair
into a collapsed atmosphere
a tube map's coloured variants
blended in black, a hoodlum lick
of couldn't care.
But it's the making, vanilla extract,
dark muscovada sugar, toffee sauce
I see folded in you, a diagram
of selectives that added to
is individually by flavour yours
like kicking a street can to see
the angle, logo-up, it falls.
We punt stories at Seven Dials
a needle obelisk, and share
the better part of what seems true,
I guess like your ingredients
go by their probability
to taste. London's so big I say
you'd have to squeeze it through your arteries
300 billion times and still find more
to know the place. You'd like to give me some
next time you bake your sweetspot stuff
and look, the light turns orange finding us.

BITS AND PIECES

Dandelions big as my fist
yellow as Selfridge's carrier
or photons popping from the sun
the same one seen out
our aqua Toyota's window
unlike the cosmic microwave background
light stretched for 13.8 billion years
and back of it a black platform.
If I wear black Converse All Star
it's to celebrate Charles Olson's
adopted brand footwear
teaching projective verse at Black Mountain
and because I dance on each word
like a ruby sequin.
I've an app on my phone to the stars
the rocky asteroid off-worlders
and I'd like an app to dead friends
to relocate a kindness
I don't often find in the living
like a never ending jar of honey.
And somewhere we stop for tea
that I think of as chasing a dragon
shaped like China and dandelions
are still full on in the present,
yellow as lemon drizzle
I eat for its compressed flavour
creating sensory dazzle.

SPLEEN AFTER BAUDELAIRE (CANNIBAL REMIX)

A grey oppressive sky's drizzled diamond
same colour as my zonked depressive down
gets under my skin, crawling on the floor –
I ask you sister/mister what a state
I'd fuck a cannibal to get a date.

The Earth rotates as a galactic cell:
I thought a bat was in my room last night
beating its fragile wings against the wall
I ask you sister/mister what a state
I'd fuck a cannibal to get a date.

Slow rain arrives of course; I see spiders
as crawling wrigglies I hallucinate,
my brain's disordered and dysfunctional
I ask you sister/mister what a state
I'd fuck a cannibal to get a date.

Suddenly sirens screams into the day
slicing the city with emergency
gutting my quarter with rapid response:
I ask you sister/mister what a state
I'd fuck a cannibal to get a date.

My window frames a black funeral limo.
somebody's there before me as a stiff
and all day I'm obsessed with how I'll die;
I ask you sister/mister what a state
I'd fuck a cannibal to get a date.

LAST TANGO

DOUGHNUT

A sugared Jovian moon
a jam dollop like a soap dispenser's
at the core a raspberry
caldera – you can bite on redemption
or do tantric sex
with the ellipsoid, the pit's
a juicy red bubble reward
a viscously compact ruby.
Used to watch John Balance shave these
2 on a plate, 2 missing,
the solo was a third
duped himself was the first,
the sugar pops substituting for booze,
a doughnut intermission
before slamming Polish vodka
with a green tint in it almost aqua
like a wave collapsed at Weston
into a drizzled prism.
A head fall over
the first floor onto slabbed marble
did for John – one-hour life-support
his brain a flopped doughnut;
and totally avoid them seeing ends
in the dusted curve's red bruise showing on a plate.

RED CARPET
lyric for Marc Almond

There's a strip of red carpet
at the top of the stair
if you go to the bottom
the red fabric's worn bare
like an old velvet jacket
gone into disrepair

I've stayed in four star and five
oodles of scarlet pile
you can die in a small town
but the end demands style
and a lover so much younger
tomorrow's in his smile

The sunset grows redder
it's like neon over Soho
it's pollution but seems
like slicing a tomato
I remember a red room
where you went in and out solo

There's a strip of red carpet
it runs out at the end
if you get to the bottom
you might find a friend
but the red carpet's ruined
in ways you can't mend

I've been up I've been down
the red plush like a sunset
it brings privilege and pain
room service and regret
and a friend at the bottom
I can't ever forget.

FALLING APART

My mother's house: I claim her pink bedroom
like I'm on Alpha Centauri
my host galaxy lost in redshift dust.
I make a writing island on her bed
that's splashy floral and green windowed mist

comes from a sky that's like a glitter ball.
Her stripped collections await house clearance –
books, teddy bears, jungle clutter, a tip
of unapproachables, mashed amalgam
I break down if I separate and stop.

She lived for things and they've outlived her now,
blank, depersonalised, dumb ephemera –
a bear's marmalade-orange zombie eyes.
I'd scramble my brain looking at the lot.
I can't make order and give up on my tries.

She fell apart and the house dipped under,
only the hyperactive jade bathroom
almost neon green holds up as a wow.
I come back periodically, don't sell,
keep on delaying, I'm frozen somehow

into suspension, her gone isn't real
as long as I imagine her alive
as near-death astronaut. I worry, clear,
campari pink roses do nods outside
I've never believed in wish you were here.

YOU'RE NOW AND THEN

Tremendous surges of black geometry
I look out over the grey shells of stores
John Lewis, Debenhams, Fraser –
concrete money blocks, monoliths
like history of my times I see don't own
under a grey cone of polluted light.
What then? Another Friday afternoon's
systemic agenda: your bare toes dexterously
tickling my face, transient brush
with sensuality. A floor sighting
of city chunks like cyber Mars bars,
your black hair cut short and spiky
as incidental, and all my silent
exotic approximations of you
you couldn't know, like what happens next door
exists on another planet, so close
it's exo. A day dipped into suspense,
no resolution, low cloud down again
it gets that silver, visibility
knocked out, hot tang of coffee, this and that,
your toes painted caramel over nude.

FINAL AUDIT

Left on the kitchen table, green Cazal's,
mint-green Perspex frames, cloud-tinted lenses
a post-dated elegy for J. H. Prynne
stored as a tablespoon of particle clusters
suspended in liquid memory.
Red fellatio-inspired graffiti
juiced with a marker on the bathroom walls:
it reads CRASHED in Coptic twizzles
like drunk dyslexia
luridly signposting a fall
a hole right through the centre of the world.
Next door's a mundane continuity –
a leather belt of bacon frying up,
a white house like a permanent Sunday
in the financial district. His boyfriend's
left with the signs – a woman in his life
anonymised like medical data –
so many subterranean psychic bends
in character, but still he'll take him back
and that crazy yellow laburnum by the wall
keeps shaking drizzled tassels like striptease.

YOU COULD BE MINE ALL MINE

It's on the back of a cereal box
close-in moon of a giant planet
concave moment shaking granola fists
into a dark blue bowl – the pathway out
for migrant species – breakfast product packaging
I like the colours, ochre, taupe and white,
the nutrient table of energies.
Out of the foam, emergent for the day,
you've got a heart-shaped ass, right side up,
point at the bottom, courtesy Lee jeans,
a dreamy indolent levitation
coming alive with juiced vivacity
acne scar on the right cheek like a pit
in which to slot an amethyst.
We're waiting on time that won't wait for us
to get away. The country first, the moon,
there's no support the further out and where?
Thundery, equinoctial slammed showers
go over – we can never know it right
the place we're headed, dig the spoon in deep
granola's like the warring of planets.

SEPTEMBER GOLD

A sunset like exploded pomegranate juice –
yesterday and today's vermilion dawn
I got it full on – Mars a red nation
(2050) – industrial resource
systemic approximation –
and look it's hung up black one-piece swimsuit
a perforated hole above the hip
on a stringy pink bathroom line.
You stay with me, separated by worlds,
three nations in your blood, black push up bra
filling out a blue angora sweater
and all I do is write compressed lyric
ignoring you, me on a word-island
as solo occupant: it has to be that way
like extra-terrestrial radio,
me submerged by a paint job, twenty coats
of hand-rubbed lacquer, locked into cut-off.
And gold September light it's like a catch,
tangible, curvy, cupped into my hand,
that generous, luxurious, so rounded-out full
of spatial travel directly from the sun.

ELIOT + 100

A century on you're colour-coded in
brown fog and river, violet hour
(request purple) like deep-throated exhaust
The Waste Land big as Battersea Power Station remake
a sort of hologrammed holistic brain
for those in know, and always near future –
a London vacuumed into end of time
pop-up apocalypse tanked into hot
nuclear currency. What of the man?
The black Oxford brogues, dumpy suits
formalised out of significant detail,
a Bloomsbury look that never met update
like sepia-fade to personality,
a cig always noodling impurities.
A boardroom milieu, a top-down view,
and yet your scrambled nerves on Margate sands
imported east capital into west
like raw language in a juicer, you got
the transcript like a culture imposter,
the city's warring genome fucked by class/race.
'London Bridge is falling down, falling down'
you got it 15,000 tonnes,
the poem like a clause in human rights
sanctioned Boni & Liveright 1922.

FOGGY ABSTRACTIONS

Moves in like undercover spook
a white parabolic umbrella
a puffy stable cloud deck
on condensation nuclei, a loop
dusting Heron Tower, Canada Square, Canary Wharf,
Leadenhall Building, Barclays, Broadgate Tower,
like a white edge worn Oxford shirt
London river fog fingerbrushed silver
like a vaporous jellyfish
slopes into circulation
over river shimmer, a green
like combats with muddy grey
and it's an aquatic aura
like an asymmetric
halo does it for me –
trekking into a no-zone
interzone between what I think
and see, like memory traces
documenting a movie
in which most of me goes missing
into cloned reality,
and fog in its blue invasive
swirly transitioning keeps up
its trophy memorabilia
like a city-sized green flash opal ring.

BOOK HOARDING

They're solid like architecture
skyscraper clusters at Canary Wharf
Canada Water
and I'm code-breaker operative
to their cryptic issue points
I buy and sell like drugs
or hoard as bankable personals
asymmetric stacks in dust-jacket condoms
like sweet wrappers, some light edgewear
or tears like a leggy girl's tights
ripped as sexualized fetish
and book smell you sniff by decades
as generational binder's glue
a musty tang like Tortilla chips
a double malt or a pissy alley's
difficultly angled corner
and they build like a mini-converted
Chelsea Waterfront as frontier
I pull from to read, evaluate
or re-order,
objects I can't let go
2,000 meditative tantric yogis
insulating me soundlessly as snow.

NO RESTING POINT (MAN, YOU GOTTA MOVE)

Dissociative, wiped, don't want it back
the past like a photo thumbprint
on consciousness – what I did's
like someone cut out of a wrecked BMW
metal pitted in close brain injuries:

that fort you rented at rocky Anneport
jade waters smashing up boulders
a fog-hazed viewpoint over Normandy
and what it started – blonde Tina OD'd
on benzos stolen from your doctor's bag

as countermeasure to your new affair.
Perrier-Jouët as a frothy aftertaste
to hitting bottom. Skinny twenty I
did every anti-anxiety sweet
you gave me – sat out on a block jetty

looking for myself four light years from home
at approx gold-filtered Centauri.
I watched the sunset saturate scarlet
into eruptive strawberry wave-lengths:
the shock of living hit me like a g.

I never found right sweetie to revise
my deficit, sank Islay scotch, waited
for life to start sheltered by Anneport fort
as cut-off point, no neighbours but stacked clouds
building again into a purple cone.

BORDEAUX SUPÉRIEUR

Displaces angles on reality,
first glass rounds edginess, tones down
jumpy bare-wired anxiety –
Château Champ de Fleuret, Moulin De Clotte,
Talian Lagrave, spiral pour

twisting a red rose in the glass
a black destablised rhomboid
got in bloodstream as brain reward.
First bite goes deepest, sugar whack
second and third go validate

pacing a bottle down to half
and fixing on the label crest
like an accessorized gold tooth.
Wine's got sunny intelligence
hot intergalactic signals

popping in crimson density.
I need this metabolic hike
like shifting floor a level up
in a department store, no drink
ever appears to hit the top.

I do it slowly, navigate
chemical changes on the way
to some point I'm almost at,
darkness outside, blue deepening night
curved like a belt around my flat.

13/2

Don't ever own to it
Aquarian arrival day – the blank
I place on owning up to age
as algorithm in my genes
biomarkers written in marker pen
don't see anyone, tell it on:
buy myself purple Afro hyacinths
from medicated blue-eyed John
like a sellophaned paint tube
and the day's damp unliftable haze
in undifferentiated grey arcs
like pencilled eyebrows.
So much gets disinformed – I can't think back
further than a one-serve scuffed tennis ball
put out of play into deep space.
My friends and fans, not one I'd call,
instead go to Penhaligon
choose Juniper Sling to up ambience
on better days: write this poem
as what my mother gave me – poetry
to lyricize both down and up
like biting on a lemon for immediacy.

Z

The female Scott
inimitable hysterical Zelda
trashy flapper rinsed by cocktails
like a Neopolitan thunder sky
champagne fizzing the colour bomb
to hallucinated supernova
deep south Alabama
liberated at 18 to Scott's
libidinous delusional binges
partying all night in Paris
the pink dawn like walking into a wall
to sober in a shredded Patou dress
as prototype Top Shop.
Banged her size 4 feet dancing
to bandaged bruised mangos
Russian pop as pheromones
to schizophrenic episodes
and the 10 star epoch novel
Save Me the Waltz
Charles Scribner's 1932
plumed hot as rocket exhaust
still the leader of the pack
an undisputed out there great
bulletish as Sylvia Plath
a time-slip casualty travelling behind her book
fetching five thousand dollars in first state.

GOING DOWN

But there's no bottom
top-down down-top like a drinker's
habituation to a loop
a need that can't be satisfied
without a need, my drop's
into a black marble gym
or subterranean observation bay
behind a concrete pillar
smells like a Boeing toilet
a stainless steel hangover
in a frying pan
it's a solo atrium
don't meet nobody down there
there's an optional clothes rail
pick out individual wear
good and bad demand a look.
It's sometime visits, once a week
I'm in a place I develop
as personalised, know its corners
where a red carpet rucks
like a scarlet trifle
and the walls are written on by me
autonomously in the dark
with silver marker, can't share its
visible invisibility
in my slow searching for a red exit.

MARTYN

A freaky local storm, you ran outside
irrationally, sky a purple lagoon
a sort of black banana holograph
over tip of north Kensington
rain smashing like Wimbledon-aced tennis balls,
your red-bobbed sister, Catherine, scrambling knobbed
asparagus spears into an omelette,
irrepressible mania in your mad
projective launch into a puddled yard,
your pink shirt flattened to you, a drenched curve
rucked at the ribs, garden table and chairs
slashed by the slam, and you peeled off your shirt
impulsively, defiantly, your hair
streaming from curls to mess, a panicked look
in thrown aggressive shapes liberating
some crisis, like emotional scar tissue,
a deep river unresolved trapped-in-you
anxiety, and came back in a pool,
rain-shocked and told us you were positive,
diagnosed HIV, poured back mashed hair,
shook yourself into our reality,
a thunder slurry rumbling in the air.